GEOGRAPHY OF CANADA

by Beth Geiger

Table of Contents

Introduction

What is **geography**? Geography is a science that deals with the study of Earth's surface and elements such as climate. Landscape and climate often affect the way people live. This book will explore the geography of Canada.

Canada has an area of about 3.8 million square miles (9.8 square kilometers). It is the largest country in North America, and the second-largest country in the world.

When you think of Canada, what comes to mind? Snow and ice? Lakes and rivers? Perhaps Canada reminds you of rugged coastlines, tall mountains, or open plains. Canada's landscape has all of those features and more.

Geography is the key to understanding Canada's people and economy. Canada may be the second-largest country in the world, but it ranks only thirty-fifth in population. About thirty-three million people live in Canada. A person can travel great distances in the northern regions without seeing anyone else. The landscape and climate make it hard to live in some areas.

Europeans first arrived in what is now Canada hundreds of years ago. They built towns and cities, usually near lakes and rivers. They also settled near natural resources, such as forests.

The way those first people settled still affects life in Canada today. Read on to discover how and why.

POINT

Talk About It
What do you want to know about Canada? With a partner, make a list of questions. Go over the list together after you have finished the book. Put a check mark beside any questions that are answered in the book.

▲ One of the largest bodies of water in Canada is Hudson Bay. It is named after Henry Hudson, who explored the bay in 1610.

Physical Geography of Canada

From coast to coast, Canada measures about 7,400 miles (11,900 kilometers). It borders the Atlantic Ocean in the east. The Pacific Ocean forms the country's western border. To the north, Canada borders the Arctic Ocean. The country is divided into ten provinces. A province is similar to a state in the United States. Much of Canada is still undeveloped wilderness.

Canada includes many different geographical regions. Each region has its own features. Far to the north are vast areas of **tundra**. Tundra is a cold, treeless area. The soil under the surface stays frozen all year. Canada also contains seven percent of the world's fresh water. Lakes and rivers can be found throughout the country.

Thousands of years ago, glaciers covered nearly all of Canada. Glaciers are thick sheets of ice. As they melted, they scoured and shaped the land. Most of the glaciers are gone, but we still see their effects in each region of the country.

Atlantic: Ocean and Mountains

Eastern Canada borders the Atlantic Ocean. It is so far east that some areas are closer to Europe than to the rest of Canada!

The Atlantic provinces used to be part of the Appalachian Mountains. Over time, the area wore down. Even so, many parts are rocky and hilly. The coastline has tall cliffs, inlets, and coves.

Some places also have **fjords** (fee-YORDZ). A fjord is a type of inlet. Inland, there are forests, farms, and swamps. Swamps are areas of wet, spongy ground.

It's a Fact

The narrow Bay of Fundy is between New Brunswick and Nova Scotia. Tides rise higher here than anywhere else in the world. Sometimes they reach nearly 60 feet (18 meters). People use the power of the big tides to make electricity. It creates enough electricity for 4,500 homes.

◀ Canada has the longest coastline in the world. It stretches 125,567 miles (202,080 kilometers). Driving the entire length would be like driving around Earth five times!

Central: Rivers, Lakes, and Lowlands

The Saint Lawrence Lowlands make up much of the southern area of central Canada. A lowland is a region of low, flat land. The Saint Lawrence River flows through parts of the lowlands. Over time, the river deposited rich soil on the flat plain.

Although the lowlands are mostly flat, a line of hills crosses the area. The hills contain rich mineral deposits. Scattered forests also grow in the region.

Central Canada borders the shores of four Great Lakes: Lake Ontario, Lake Erie, Lake Huron, and Lake Superior. The lakes were formed by melting glaciers. The water from Lake Ontario flows into the Saint Lawrence River. In the winter, the Saint Lawrence River and parts of the Great Lakes freeze.

Math Matters

In Canada, distances on roads and maps are measured in kilometers. One mile equals about 1.6 kilometers. You might hear a Canadian refer to a distance in "clicks." That is a nickname for kilometers.

▲ the Great Lakes as seen from space

The northern part of central Canada is part of the Canadian Shield. The Canadian Shield is a vast rock base. It is made up of some of Earth's oldest rocks. The shield lies under almost half of Canada. It has greatly affected the landscape of the country.

Most of the Canadian Shield is a rolling, rocky **plateau** (pla-TOH). Parts of the Canadian Shield are covered with forests, swamps, and lakes. Other parts are treeless.

Hudson Bay is another important natural feature of the area. Hudson Bay is an inland sea. It is connected to the Atlantic and Arctic Oceans. James Bay extends south from Hudson Bay like a big toe.

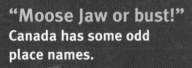

"Moose Jaw or bust!"
Canada has some odd place names.

In a giggly mood?
Head for Ha Ha Bay in Newfoundland. It's an old French term for a dead end.

Don't forget Moose Jaw.
The name could be from the Cree word *moosegaw*, which means "warm breezes."

And for a real in-your-face kind of place, it's not far from **Moose Jaw** to **Eyebrow**.

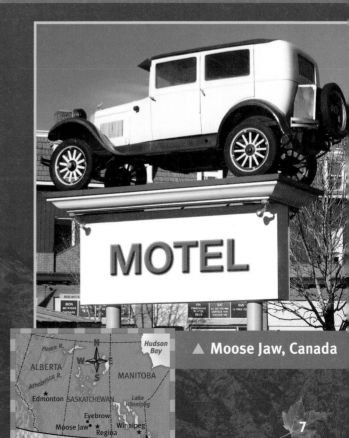

▲ Moose Jaw, Canada

7

West: From Prairies to Mountains

Western Canada includes wide-open prairies. Prairies are mostly flat, but they do have hills in some areas. Much of the prairie soil came from sediment left behind from glaciers and rivers. The soil is highly fertile.

The climate in the prairies is extreme. Winters are very cold and windy. Summers are very hot.

Forested wilderness stretches north of the prairies. The area also contains many lakes. In fact, water covers almost one-sixth of this region. Most of the lakes were carved out of the Canadian Shield by glaciers. The biggest lake is Lake Winnipeg. It is 266 miles (428 kilometers) long.

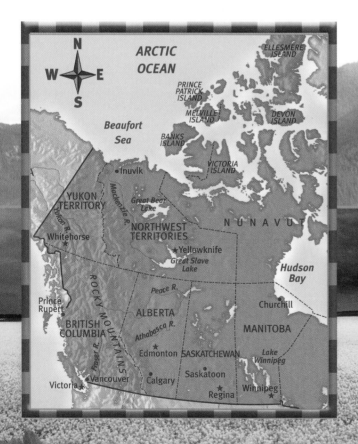

You can find plains like this in Saskatchewan. ▲

The dry, grassy plains of the prairies gradually slope up to the west. They end about 2,000 feet (610 meters) above sea level. Then the Rocky Mountains rise abruptly above the plains. The Coast Range, covered in glaciers, lies still farther west. Between the two ranges are high, dry valleys.

Western coastal areas have Canada's wettest and mildest climate. Just offshore, Vancouver Island is the wettest place in North America. Parts of the island receive as much as 262 inches (665 centimeters) of rain each year. The region is home to a **temperate** (TEM-puh-rit) rain forest. The rainy climate makes it possible for some of the biggest trees on Earth to grow there.

Western Canada's wet coast and its dry mountain valleys aren't that far apart. Why are they so different? The coastal mountains block Pacific Ocean moisture from reaching the eastern side of the mountains. This is called the rain shadow effect.

They Made a Difference

David Thompson helped map Canada. He traveled around western Canada from 1797 to 1826. Everywhere he went, he drew maps. Thompson was very good at calculating distances and locations. Because of this, his maps were called "astonishingly accurate." Altogether, he traveled more than 50,000 miles (80,467 kilometers).

North: Extremes and Surprises

Much of far northern Canada is icy wilderness. Glaciers covered this land only 10,000 years ago. The area has the coldest temperatures and harshest landscape in Canada. In the north, rivers and lakes are frozen all winter.

Much of the north is too cold for trees to grow. The tree line marks the northern limit of forests. Beyond the tree line, the climate is too extreme for trees. The treeless landscape there is tundra.

The tundra region is called the Barrenlands. Despite this forbidding name, the Barrenlands is home to caribou and other wildlife.

Northern Climates

Town	Elevation	Latitude	Average July Temperature	Average January Temperature
Whitehorse, Yukon	2,300 feet (701 meters)	60°N	57.2°F (14°C)	1°F (−18.3°C)
Yellowknife, NWT	670 feet (204 meters)	62°N	61.2°F (16.2°C)	−18.1°F (−27.8°C)
Iqaluit, Nunavut	110 feet (33.5 meters)	63.75°N	15.9°F (8.9°C)	−14.7° (−25.9°C)F

Glaciers left their mark on the treeless land in the north. The glaciers left behind gravelly ridges called eskers. These ridges wind across the Barrenlands.

The north has few trees, but it does have a lot of water. Its largest lake is Great Slave Lake, which is about 300 miles (483 kilometers) long. The powerful Mackenzie River is Canada's longest river. It flows north from the western end of Great Slave Lake. The Mackenzie travels 1,120 miles (1,800 kilometers) and empties into the Arctic Ocean.

Not all of the north is treeless and flat. Parts of the northwest are covered by huge mountains. There are vast areas of forest there, too. Birch and spruce trees fill the large valleys.

Q&A

Permafrost (PER-muh-frost) is soil or rock that stays frozen all year. Richard Trimble is an engineer in Whitehorse, Yukon. He tells about the problems it can cause.

Q: What can happen if buildings are built on permafrost?

A: If a heated structure, such as a house, is built on top of the permafrost, the heat from the building will thaw it.

Q: What happens then?

A: The ground settles. Northern Canada has quite a few examples of buildings that have tilted or collapsed due to permafrost thaw.

▲ Canada's arctic tundra

Human Geography of Canada

The natural features of Canada affect where people live. Many places in the far north have harsh climates and few people. Most people like the milder climate in the south. Today, about 75 percent of Canada's population lives less than 200 miles (about 321 kilometers) from the U.S. border.

Much of inland Canada is covered by mountains and forests. This makes travel difficult. Early settlers in Canada lived along coasts and rivers. They used boats to transport goods on the water.

Atlantic: Bounty of the Sea

The waters along Newfoundland and Labrador once teemed with Atlantic cod. The rich fishery brought settlers to the coast. Today, most people still live along the ocean. The inland area of Labrador has almost no roads because so few people live there.

Shipping is very important to the region's economy. Some harbors stay ice-free all winter. That is because the salty ocean water doesn't freeze as quickly as fresh water.

Primary Source

Author L. M. Montgomery created one of Canada's most famous residents, eleven-year-old Anne. Here's an excerpt from the 1906 book *Anne of Green Gables*. It describes Prince Edward Island.

"Spring had come once more to Green Gables— the beautiful, capricious, reluctant Canadian spring, lingering along through April and May in a succession of sweet, fresh, chilly days, with pink sunsets and miracles of resurrection and growth. Away up in the barrens . . . the Mayflowers blossomed out, pink and white stars of sweetness . . . 'I'm so sorry for people who live in lands where there are no Mayflowers,' said Anne."

Central: Where the Crowds Are

Central Canada is the country's most populated region. More than 60 percent of Canadians live there.

Why? You could say it's the water. Early French settlers traveled up the Saint Lawrence River. They established cities that grew into main trade and transportation centers. Now trucks and trains bring crops from inland Canada to port cities. The goods are then loaded onto ships that export Canadian goods all over the world.

Settled in the 1700s, Toronto is on the north shore of Lake Ontario. It is a major shipping center and Canada's largest city.

Montreal is another important city in this region. It was settled by French people in the early 1600s. More than 90 percent of the residents of Montreal still speak French as their main language.

Canada's Population Density

People per sq. mile
- □ 0 to 4
- ▨ 5 to 49
- ▧ 50 to 99
- ▩ 100 to 250
- ■ More than 250

N W E S

▲ Almost four million people live in Toronto today.

Of course, not everyone in the central region lives in big cities. There are still large areas of wilderness.

Natural resources also affected settlement. Areas of the Canadian Shield are rich in minerals, including gold, iron, copper, and lead. The Arctic area has large deposits of diamonds. Mining brought people to central and northern Canada.

Most areas in the far north are not developed. There are almost no roads. The few towns are linked by water and air travel. Many settlements in this region are home to Canada's native people. These people are called First Nations citizens because they were Canada's first residents. Major First Nations groups in the northern central region include Cree and Inuit (IH-noo-wut).

▲ The Inuit people were once known as Eskimos.

West: Full of Promise

The Métis (MAY-tee) are an important ethnic group in western Canada. They are people of mixed European and First Nations heritage. They've had their own way of life since the 1700s. That is when French fur traders and trappers first arrived.

The prairie covers large parts of this region. The land is fertile and good for farming. This helped attract settlers. Canada's railroad made it possible for settlers to move to the prairie. By 1880, trains connected the west with eastern Canada. People could use the trains to transport crops to sell in the east.

▲ Saskatchewan is a province famous for grains.

Parts of the prairie are also used as ranch land. The mixed grasses that grow there are ideal for feeding herds of animals. Large ranches in the area raise cattle and some even raise buffalo.

Natural resources also helped early people settle along Canada's west coast. The thick forests provided a large supply of wood. People also came to hunt. Animal meat was used for food. The furs were sold.

The largest city on the west coast is Vancouver. It began as the end of the railways from the east. The city has become an important trade gateway. Forest products, grains, and other goods are loaded on ships bound for Asia. At the same time, ships arrive loaded with cars and other goods.

It's a Fact

British Columbia refused to join Canada until it was promised a railroad to connect it to the rest of the nation. Easier said than done! Building a railroad across the rugged Rocky Mountains was tough.

For twenty-five years, trains careened out of control on the steep tracks at Kicking Horse Pass. Then, engineers had a solution. In 1909, they built two spiral tunnels into the mountainside. This made the tracks longer and less steep. Now trains cross the Rocky Mountains more easily and safely.

North: A Special Beauty

Canada's north holds special beauty for the people that live there. There are large mountains, many lakes, and areas of forested wilderness. At times, the northern lights color the sky. The northern lights are caused when particles from the sun get caught in Earth's magnetic field.

Many settlers first came to the north when gold was discovered in 1896. They came to a region called the Klondike, along the Yukon River. Gold-seekers quickly built many towns. Many of the towns no longer exist, but Whitehorse and Yellowknife still thrive as centers for gold and diamond mining. Those towns are also busy regional capitals.

Primary Source

A headline in the July 17, 1897, issue of the *White Pass Chronicle* announced the discovery of gold in northern Canada. The news encouraged thousands to seek their fortunes there. In 1900, $22 million in gold was mined in the area.

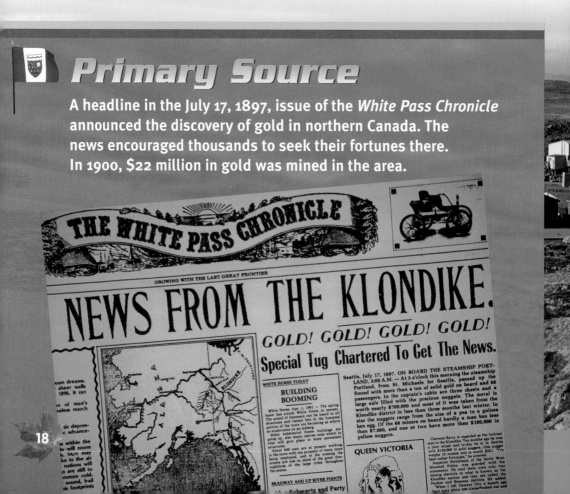

Nunavut (NOO-nuh-voot) was established in 1999 as an Inuit homeland. Eighty-five percent of its residents are Inuit. For thousands of years, the Inuit have survived in the harsh landscape. The Inuit have strong cultural traditions. Fur clothing, igloos, and dogsleds are all part of the Inuit way of life.

Today, most Inuit do not follow ancient ways. Even so, some still hunt and fish for their food in traditional ways.

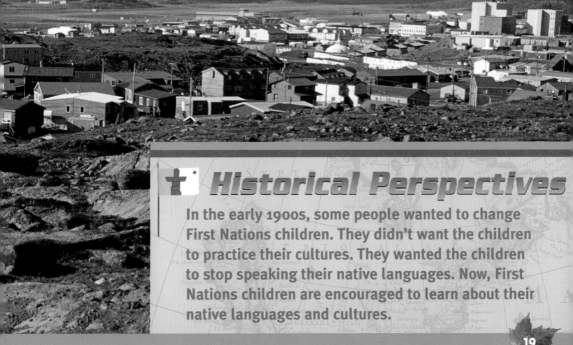

✦ *Historical Perspectives*

In the early 1900s, some people wanted to change First Nations children. They didn't want the children to practice their cultures. They wanted the children to stop speaking their native languages. Now, First Nations children are encouraged to learn about their native languages and cultures.

▲ **Iqaluit (ee-KAH-loo-ut) on Baffin Island is the capital of Nunavut.**

Canada's Resources and Economy

Canada's geography shapes its economy. Different areas of the country provide different natural resources, such as oil, lumber, gold, and diamonds. The natural resources bring wealth to Canada.

Canada meets its own needs, and also creates a wide range of products to sell to other countries. It exports products that range from wheat to **hydroelectric power** (HI-droh-ih-LEK-trik POW-er). Hydroelectric power is created by harnessing the flow of rivers. To do this, people build dams across rivers. Water flows through machines called turbines in the dams. The turbines generate electricity. The electricity is sent long distances through power lines.

▲ **This is the La Grande hydroelectric power station in Quebec. It's the world's largest hydroelectric power plant.**

Atlantic: Fish to Forests

Most areas of the Atlantic were settled for the fishing along the coast. Fishing is still the region's most important business. Canada exports 75 percent of its fish.

For centuries, many people earned a living by fishing for cod. By 1993, there weren't many cod left. The government decided to stop cod fishing so that the cod population would have a chance to grow. People can still catch other types of fish along the Atlantic coast.

Logging is another important business. Thick forests along the coast are the source for products ranging from ship masts to plywood.

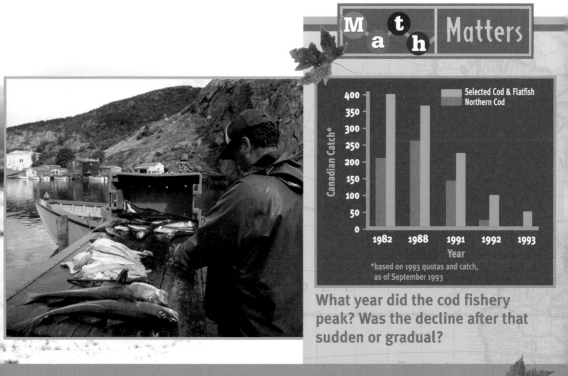

Math Matters

What year did the cod fishery peak? Was the decline after that sudden or gradual?

▲ Many people lost their jobs when the government put a stop to cod fishing.

Central: Canada's Economic Heart

Most of Canada's businesses are found in the central part of the country. Would this be true without some important geographic features? The answer is no.

The transportation routes of the Great Lakes and the Saint Lawrence River are key to the region's trade. Ships carry goods from the middle of Canada and the United States all the way to Europe and Asia.

Manufacturing plants in the area depend on hydroelectric power from fast-flowing rivers up north. This has made the western shore of Lake Ontario wealthy. In fact, people have nicknamed the area The Golden Horseshoe.

▲ Boats travel the 28-mile-long (44-kilometer-long) Welland Canal to get around Niagara Falls into Lake Erie.

Natural transportation routes are keys to the region's success. The Saint Lawrence Seaway is a system of canals and navigation locks. This route uses the region's big rivers and lakes.

All the lakes and rivers aren't at the same water level. The locks raise and lower ships. They make it possible for ships to travel between large bodies of water. The locks also allow oceangoing ships to travel far inland. Without the locks, ships could not pass the towering Niagara Falls.

▲ Niagara Falls

◀ Thousand Islands Bridge crosses the Saint Lawrence River. The bridge connects Ontario and New York.

It's a Fact

About 1.85 billion years ago, a comet slammed into the area that is now Sudbury. It punched out a crater 155 miles (250 kilometers) in diameter. The comet contained millions of tons of copper and nickel. The metals were left in the crater.

23

West: Grain, Cattle, Oil, and Trees

Geography determines the economy of western Canada. Farming is an important business. The rich prairie soils have created one of the world's finest grain-growing regions. People process the grains for work. They also raise livestock on farms and ranches.

Lake Winnipeg also gives people on the prairies the chance to make a living from fishing and shipping. To the north, the city of Churchill is Canada's only port on the Arctic Ocean. It provides a shorter route for shipping the region's grains to Europe and Africa. Churchill's port is only open three months per year because of ice.

In 1947, oil was discovered in Alberta. Today, the province produces enough petroleum to export to the United States. Alberta also has a great deal of coal. It sells large amounts of the coal to Japan.

▲ Canadian wheat is shipped to more than seventy countries.

Along Canada's west coast, forestry is big business. The wet, mild climate creates dense forests. Some of the biggest trees on Earth grow in the region. Many people work in logging and sawmill operations.

The coast also provides many ports and places to fish. Salmon are some of the most important fish in this area.

Geography has helped the west coast in another way. The beautiful landscape and mild climate attract many visitors. People travel from all over the world to see the area's waterfalls and rain forests. Tourism grows every year. People also enjoy sport fishing, skiing, boating, and hiking. They spend their money at local businesses, helping the economy to grow.

In My Opinion

In 1972, Canada began building the James Bay hydroelectric project in northern Quebec. The project was partly completed. Then it was put on hold. Historian Alan MacEachern explains the arguments for and against the project.

Pro: "Prior to the project, people in the area were quite poor. The project has made their land more valuable, provided them with opportunities to do other jobs, and has given them more contact with the outside world."

Con: "The project changed ecosystems and disrupted where animals and even fish can live. The Cree and Inuit people who lived in the area were greatly affected by the project. In some cases, their homes were flooded. Also, even if the people's own land was not flooded, fish and animals they relied on for food and trade were no longer where they had always been. Because of these things many Cree and Inuit had to move. Some worry that the project will make it harder for the Cree and Inuit to maintain their traditional culture."

25

North: The Lure of Minerals

Minerals are the force behind northern Canada's economy. Some people mine gold. Others mine lead, zinc, and diamonds. Oil is another important resource.

It's not easy to mine those resources in the remote Barrenlands. Workers must be flown in and housed at the mines. It is difficult to heat a large mining camp in the frozen tundra.

Also, supplies are expensive to transport. Trucks bring the biggest equipment in during winter, when they can drive across the frozen swamps and lakes. All those factors make mining tough and expensive. Even so, the mines and oil wells are valuable to northern Canada's economy.

✔ POINT

Picture It
Draw a picture that illustrates the information on this page. Then write a caption that explains why the miners and oil field workers are willing to face these types of hardships.

Nunavut is different. Most people there still catch or hunt their food. Because of this, Nunavut does not have the same type of balanced trade as other Canadian regions.

Nunavut also faces special transportation challenges. There are almost no roads outside the small towns. Even if the distances weren't so great, the terrain is rugged. Imagine trying to build roads across a land that has thousands of lakes and swamps! Instead, most communities are on the coast. Air travel is a way of life.

In Their Own Words

The Alaska Highway is an important route across the Yukon. During World War II, the U.S. Army built the 1,400-mile-long (2,253-kilometer-long) Alaska Highway in just eight months. Wallace Lytle helped build it.

"The mud made it hard to bring in equipment. . . ." explained Lytle. "The tires would build up so much mud . . . they (would) just slide right off the road."

The mosquitoes were terrible, too. "You just had to wear head nets," Mr. Lytle remembered. Ice also caused big problems. In the fall, crews were building a bridge across the Peace River. "The ice broke up and took out three or four hundred feet of that bridge," Lytle said.

▲ Some northern supply roads exist only in the winter, when trucks can be driven across the frozen lakes and swamps.

Conclusion

Canada is just one country, but it has many different landscapes. There are the frozen Barrenlands, and there are dense rain forests. There are towering mountain peaks, and there are prairies as flat as a table. Canada is dry and wet, gentle and harsh.

The geography offers many choices for the people of Canada. Some choose to live in large cities along major waterways. Others prefer small towns in the prairies or the far north.

Canada's resources have helped to create many kinds of jobs for its people. Forests have fueled a busy paper and wood product industry. Minerals have made mining a big business. Hydroelectric energy from rivers powers many plants.

▲ These workers are cutting down trees to send to Canada's paper mills.

Yet even today, large parts of Canada remain undeveloped wilderness. There may be many more resources in those areas waiting to be found. Canada is an interesting country with a unique landscape. In the past, its geography has shaped how and where people settled. Geography will continue to affect the people who live in Canada far into the future.

▲ **Many tourists enjoy Canada's wilderness.**

1608	A French fur-trading post is built in what later becomes Quebec.
1642	Montreal is founded and becomes a fur-trading center.
1670	The Hudson's Bay Company establishes fur-trading posts, such as Moose Factory on Hudson Bay, and begins major exploration of western and northern Canada.
1867	Canada is established as a nation separate from British colonies.
1885	The Canadian Pacific Railway is completed. It was a crucial link to settlement of the prairie provinces and the addition of British Columbia to Canada.
1898	Gold is discovered in the Yukon. The Klondike gold rush begins; it is the biggest gold rush in history.
1942	The Alaska Highway is built. It connects communities in the Yukon.

1959	The Saint Lawrence Seaway opens.
1962	The Trans-Canada Highway opens, forming a continuous auto road from coast to coast.
1972	The James Bay hydroelectric project begins.
1993	The government declares a stop to most cod fishing in Newfoundland.
1998	A diamond mine is opened in the Northwest Territories north of Yellowknife.
1999	Nunavut is created as an Inuit homeland (separated from Northwest Territories).

Glossary

fjord	(fee-YORD) an inlet of the ocean, usually caused by flooding of a glacial valley (page 5)
geography	(jee-AH-gruh-fee) study of Earth's features in a particular place (page 2)
hydroelectric power	(HI-droh-ih-LEK-trik POW-er) power generated by rivers (page 20)
plateau	(pla-TOH) high, somewhat flat area of land (page 7)
temperate	(TEM-puh-rit) having a mild climate (page 9)
tundra	(TUN-druh) treeless plain of Arctic regions (page 4)

Index